T0156894

Maria the Panther

Chronicle of the Twentieth Century

Adam Adrian Brostow

iUniverse, Inc.
New York Bloomington

Maria the Panther
Chronicle of the Twentieth Century

iUniverse books may be ordered through booksellers or by contacting:

iUniverse
1663 Liberty Drive
Bloomington, IN 47403
www.iuniverse.com
1-800-Authors (1-800-288-4677)

Because of the dynamic nature of the Internet, any Web addresses or links contained in this book may have changed since publication and may no longer be valid. The views expressed in this work are solely those of the author and do not necessarily reflect the views of the publisher, and the publisher hereby disclaims any responsibility for them.

ISBN: 978-1-4502-3993-6 (sc)
ISBN: 978-1-4502-3994-3 (ebook)
ISBN: 978-1-4502-3995-0 (dj)

Printed in the United States of America

iUniverse rev. date: 8/11/2010

Contents

Introduction

This is the story of my grandmother. I hope it will be of interest to many. I think it transcends boundaries and cultures.

My grandma Maria was born in 1902 in Warsaw, at that time part of the Russian empire. She died in 1992 at the age of eighty-nine in free Poland. She survived WWI. She cheated death at least four times during WWII. She was arrested by the Soviet NKVD (later known as the KGB). As private, serial number 202, Home Army, she fought the Nazis in the Resistance and the Warsaw Uprising.

She was taken to a Nazi concentration camp and later worked at a labor camp in Berlin. There she gained a nickname, "The Panther," for her resourcefulness and courage. She survived the carpet bombing of Berlin.

In the late 1940s, at a time when most women were confined to domestic duties, she became president of a bank. She lived to see the fall of the Berlin Wall.

She was full of contradictions. A practicing Catholic, she believed in reincarnation. A Socialist before WWII under a right-wing government, she became a soldier of the right-leaning Home Army during the war. After the war she was a member of the ruling Socialist Party in Communist Poland. Eventually, she joined the anticommunist Solidarity Trade Union in her retirement.

Grandma spoke Russian and German flawlessly and knew French. When I was a child, she spoke and sang to me in all those languages. She hunted wild boar, swore, told jokes that could make a sailor blush, and drank her vodka straight. She taught me to play poker and blackjack.

She went hiking with me in the mountains in her mid-seventies. She taught me about flowers and animals, exotic food, and introduced me to arts and culture.

To clarify, Maria was actually not my grandmother but my grandaunt. She was my maternal grandmother's sister. However, I always called her Grandma Maria. Having no children of her own, she took care of my mother (also named Maria) when she was little, then me, then my younger sister, Eva Maria. She was a role model to all of us.

I think her life is a quintessential experience of twentieth-century Europe. It can also be a handbook on how to lead a healthy, productive life and still have lots of fun. I feel it's my duty to tell her story.

With racism and xenophobia still an issue in Europe, the U.S., and elsewhere, my grandma's story illustrates how arbitrary the concept of race really is. A white European, during the Nazi occupation of Poland she was considered to be of an inferior race and confined to the back of a streetcar.

Her story talks about good Poles and bad Poles, good Germans and bad Germans, good Russians and bad Russians. Many people tend to attribute good or bad characteristics to entire national, ethnic, or religious groups without looking at each person as a unique individual.

I apologize for the simple, unembellished style of my story and possible historical and factual inaccuracies. It is based on what my grandma told me when I was between seven and fifteen years old and on recollections from my childhood. I cannot add details because they would be untrue to the original story.

The stories and anecdotes are episodic and self-contained. They were originally written separately and over a long period of time. It is hard to connect them into a smooth narrative as I never had a chance to interview my grandmother to fill in the gaps. They vary in length. I thought even the shortest stories and anecdotes are worth retelling.

I have been told my narrative is unconventional. Well, I don't follow conventions. I learned it from Grandma!

From my limited knowledge, I added some information about the historical and cultural background. Some of it may not be accurate. The reader is encouraged to seek more information.

I tried to avoid injecting my own opinions into the narrative, but at the risk of being called egotistical, I sometimes felt compelled to do so. The reader can always disagree.

Before WWI
The Russian Empire, later Poland,
1902–1914

First communion, Warsaw, circa 1910

Before WWI, Poland was nowhere to be found on the map of Europe. It was divided for a century and a quarter between Prussia, the Austro-Hungarian Empire, and the Russian empire.

My maternal grandparents were subjects of Czar Nicholas II of Russia. After the insurrection in the late eighteenth century and two failed uprisings in the nineteenth century, the Russians banned the Polish language in schools. Unlike the Orthodox Russians, Poles use the Roman (Latin) alphabet instead of Cyrillic and are firmly linked to the West through their Catholic faith.

In fact, the Polish language is older than Russian or English, and the united Polish state is older than Russia or Britain. Poland has the second oldest codified democratic constitution in the world, following the American constitution (or perhaps the third following America and Iceland).

My paternal grandparents were from the southern province of Galicia and, therefore, subjects of the emperor Franz Joseph I. Since Austria-Hungary was a multiethnic state and Austrians, like Poles, were predominately Catholic, the Austrian partition enjoyed relative freedom.

After a century and a quarter of oppression, Poles emerged even more defiant and rebellious and even more aware of their heritage.

Grandma Maria was born in Warsaw to Helena, a beautiful raven-haired aristocrat, and Andrzej (Andrew) who worked for the czar's railroad. Great-Grandma Helena was very strict, while Andrzej was mild-mannered and permissive.

Great-Grandma Helena wore a corset that made her waist as thin as a wasp's. When she got angry, she swore viciously in Russian. "Why can't you swear in Polish?" asked Great-Grandpa.

"I don't want to abuse my native tongue," she would reply.

Butcher
Warsaw, circa 1914

When Grandma went to elementary school for girls, right before the outbreak of WWI, pupils were only allowed to speak Russian in class. They were told they were Russian and they had to learn Russian history, literature, and tradition. The Polish language was called "a corrupt version of Russian."

Grandma actually liked her Russian teacher. Her name was Nina Vasilievna Mukha. She was a tall and beautiful woman with jet-black hair. Sixty years later Grandma could still recite to me the Russian poems taught by Nina. She would quote from memory a poem by Lermontov about the battle of Borodino. Grandma liked the poem, even though the defeat of Napoleon at Borodino meant the end of the short-lived Polish dream of independence.

Her German teacher was another story. She was a German native. If she found a dirty spot on a girl's dress, she would call her *Polnisches Schwein* (Polish pig). In a way, she was defeating the efforts of Russian authorities by reminding the girls who they were. But Grandma had to admit that the woman was an excellent teacher. Thirty years later, Grandma would use her German fluency to make her tiny contribution toward defeating the Third Reich. Her German probably saved her life.

But the girls needed no reminder of who they were. Outside of school they were all raised as Polish patriots. Great-Grandma would not allow a word of Russian spoken at home (except for her own obscenities).

Like many girls in many countries, Grandma kept a diary. One boy wrote in her diary in Polish verse: *"Dobra sztuka mięsa, jeszcze lepszy mostek. Wolę Twe usteczka bo w nich nie ma kostek."* This roughly translates: "Steak is good, spare ribs even better. I prefer your lips, because they have no bones."

Someone else, perhaps a priest, wrote in her diary: *"Za prawdę wieczne szczęście cię czeka; prawda Bóg sam. Lecz gdy masz prawdą zabić człowieka to wtedy kłam."* This translates: "Being truthful will bring you eternal happiness; truth is the God Himself. But if you were to kill a man with the truth, then lie."

Grandma always got top grades in school. There was only one time when she got the lowest grade, which was during the history lesson. The teacher asked her: "Maria Andreevna (meaning Maria, daughter of Andrew), could you tell us who Alexander Suvorov was?" The expected answer was: "A great Russian hero." However, Grandma knew a different version of history.

In 1794 Thaddeus Kościuszko led the uprising against the Russians. He was the same Kościuszko who was brigadier general in Washington's Continental Army during the American Revolution. He has monuments erected in his honor on Lafayette Square in Washington and at West Point. He also has a museum in Philadelphia. A military engineer, he designed the fortifications of West Point, Philadelphia, and Ticonderoga. The American victory at Ticonderoga was arguably the turning point of the American Revolution.

Going back to the story, the Russian General Suvorov was fighting the insurgents and was possibly responsible for the massacre of 20,000 Polish civilians, including women, children, and the elderly, in a Warsaw suburb of Praga (it's not clear whether he gave the order or simply did not prevent the Cossacks from committing the atrocities).

"He was a butcher!" my twelve-year-old Grandma blurted out. She had tears in her eyes. She was proud of that lowest grade for her entire life.

WWI
The Russian Empire, later Poland, 1914–1918

During WWI, Austria-Hungary became Prussia's ally and fought against Russia and the Western allies. Poles fought in all three armies of the occupying powers. Sometimes family members fought each other in different uniforms. My paternal grandfather, a junior lieutenant at seventeen, fought for Austria. Fortunately, none of my relatives on my mother's side were in the Russian army, or they could have faced my grandfather.

During the war, Grandma relocated with her family to the countryside. Grandma remembers the havoc caused at that time in Europe by the Spanish influenza. It was safer to live in the countryside than in the city. There was a severe shortage of teachers. At fourteen, Grandma got her first job teaching children at a rural school. She was a strict disciplinarian. She used the ruler to smack disobeying children.

I suspect that life in the country changed my Grandma's outlook on the world. She was no longer a young city girl afraid to take a cold shower or use an outhouse. She also developed her love for animals: horses, dogs, and even chickens.

After WWI, Poland was devastated but finally free. American president Woodrow Wilson presented his fourteen points before Congress. Point number thirteen talked about free Poland with access to the sea. The Allies agreed to it.

In 1920, Poland was attacked again by Russia (now the Soviet Union) after Polish forces ventured into the Ukraine. The Russians pushed them back all way to Warsaw and the Vistula River. In the battle known as Miracle at the Vistula, the Russians suffered a crushing defeat. Grandma recalled the story of a Catholic priest, Father Ignacy Jan Skorupka, who prayed for somebody like Joan of Arc to appear and save Poland. Then he led people to the battle himself. He did not live to see the victory.

Poland regained its territory as well as a part of Lithuania, Belarus, and the Ukraine, formerly parts of the Polish-Lithuanian Commonwealth. Nearly twenty years later this would provide an excuse for another Soviet invasion.

During his years working for the tsar's railroad, Great-Grandpa Andrzej amassed a small fortune in 100 and 500-ruble banknotes with the image of Empress Catherine the Great and a watermark. Half a century later, Grandma Maria still kept them in her "treasure box" and let me play with them. After WWI and the Bolshevik revolution they were worthless. They were once again just pieces of paper.

Tapeworm
Early Twentieth Century

One day, while vacationing in the countryside, Grandma went "to the bathroom" behind a barn. This was a normal way to do it. It was before the independence when one of the Polish prime ministers made it mandatory for each rural household to have an outhouse. Grandma noticed something white came out of her body. She called Great-Grandma Helena. Great-Grandma had the doctor examine the white, tapelike object. He concluded it was a tapeworm. Unfortunately, the head was missing. The doctor said it was still in the body and the tapeworm would regenerate. He prescribed some bitter medicine and advised going to the bathroom over a chamber pot containing warm milk, supposedly to lure the worm. Whether the milk worked or not, the head eventually came out.

Great-Grandma Helena also suffered from a tapeworm. Grandma Maria recalls that one day her mother started choking, and white foam appeared on her lips. Great-Grandpa Andrzej pulled out a section of a tapeworm from her mouth. I don't remember the details, but the story ended in a similar manner as the previous one.

Grandma Maria lost one of her two sisters to galloping tuberculosis. Michalina was always sickly. One day she fell and hurt herself and became confined to her bed. Within a week she was dead. She was only fourteen. Maria's other younger sister, Stefania, would become my grandmother.

Tapeworms and tuberculosis, now largely eradicated in the Western world, were common at the time.

Old Lilpop
Warsaw, 1920s

After finishing high school, Grandma studied economics at a business school. Upon graduation she was hired by the Lilpop, Rau, and Loewenstein factory in Warsaw to work in the office.

Mr. Lilpop had a pointed nose and wore wire-rimmed glasses. He also had a dog, a dachshund that accompanied him everywhere. One day Lilpop left his glasses on top of his desk. Grandma, twenty-something at the time, picked them up and put them on Lilpop's dachshund's nose. The poor dog ran like crazy through the hallways and offices with the glasses on. Office workers could not stop laughing. Everybody said the dog looked just like old man Lilpop himself.

Marriage and a New Job
Poland, 1930s

Grandma married Janek (Johnny) Podgórski, a navy officer. She said she was impressed by his well-pressed uniform and his shiny Colt Navy revolver. Her marriage introduced her to a circle of army and navy officers, horse races, whisky and soda, gambling, recreational drug use, and hunting.

Grandpa Johnny (he was obviously not my real grandfather) was quite possessive. When some man struck up a conversation with Grandma at a bar, he took a soda water siphon and sprayed the guy's face, saying: "I'll break your mug."

The officers were a rowdy bunch. They drank like fish, quarreled, and dueled. One day during a party, Grandma went to the room adjacent to the dancehall and found her husband's friend snorting powdered cocaine. Others smoked opium brought from the Far East.

About the same time, Grandma got a new job at the M. Arct Publishing Company as an accountant. She loved the beautiful albums published by Arct. Much later I learned about nature, animals, and minerals by reading those rare books that survived WWII.

Grandma Maria, 1930s

Boar Hunt
Poland, 1930s

In the 1930s, Grandma used to go hunting with her husband's friends, all men. She learned to shoot a rifle and a pistol. Once she fired in the air, in her own words, "at God's window," and a dead bird fell from the sky. At least that is what she said. My mother says Grandma "colorized" some of her less-serious stories (I don't quite believe Grandma's story about a rooster that crowed after his head got cut off).

It was during the wild boar hunt that she experienced the most danger and excitement. She did not have a gun at the time. They had been tracking the boar for a while. They could see the places where fresh earth was exposed by the boar's snout. Finally, the huge beast was cornered at a clearing in the forest. One of the men took a shot. The boar was hit, but it only roared as if possessed by a demon and started running straight at Grandma, big tusks gleaming in the sun, blood dripping from its side.

Grandma stood in place as if her feet were frozen to the ground. She remembered being advised to climb a tree in such circumstances. But she was in the middle of the clearing, and there was no tree in sight.

A second shot was fired. The boar got hit again, slowed down for a fraction of a second, and then kept coming. The adrenaline rush from anger and fear made it oblivious to pain and blood loss. Then one of the other men, an experienced hunter, took careful aim and squeezed the trigger. The boar fell as if struck by lightning.

When they examined the carcass they could not initially find the third wound. The third bullet entered through the eye, penetrated the brain, and lodged itself inside the thick skull. The experienced hunter explained that, in order to drop a beast that size, one had to hit it either in the eye or directly in the heart. Otherwise, it would only make the animal even more dangerous.

Runaway Horse
Poland, 1930s

Grandma loved to ride horses. She also went to horse races.

One day she was riding across the countryside with a group of friends when her horse bolted. He galloped through the woods and across meadows, jumping over fences, with Grandma holding on for dear life, unable to stop him or slow him down. She pressed her face to the horse's neck to avoid being hit by branches. She was very scared.

One member of her party, an experienced rider, followed her, caught up to her horse, and grabbed him by the reins. He rode alongside Grandma for a while until Grandma's horse stopped.

This incident did not prevent Grandma from riding the next day.

Dinner at the Chinese Embassy Warsaw, 1930s

Grandpa Johnny claimed he spoke several Chinese dialects, including Mandarin and Cantonese. Whether it was true or not, he knew the Chinese ambassador to Poland. The ambassador's name was Cheng Chin Fen, or at least this was how Grandma pronounced it.

One day, Fen invited Grandma to a dinner party at the embassy. First they brought the appetizer consisting of a plate of live beetles. Each Chinese took one, got ahold of the rear part, disemboweled the insect with one quick pull, opened the shell, and ate the inside. The soup was next. It looked suspicious. "Fen, what is it?" asked Grandma. "Swallows' nests?"

"Tastes good? Then eat it!" was the answer.

The soup was indeed delicious. Then the main course was served. "Fen, what is this? Dog meat?"

"Tastes good? Then eat it!" Fen said.

With the meal came Chinese tea. "Fen, do you have any sugar?" asked Grandma.

"Sure, suit yourself. But you are going to regret it."

Grandma put two spoons of sugar into a teacup. "Fen, this tastes terrible!"

"Try it without sugar," Fen suggested and gave her the "See, I told you so" look. So Grandma tried it without sugar. The tea tasted great, slightly bitter, rich in flavor, aromatic.

Ever since, Grandma never used sugar again, with tea or with coffee. She taught me the same trick. I got so used to tea without sugar that I cannot stand the sweet taste anymore.

Years later I visited China and tried boiled silkworms. I also tried fried grasshoppers and agave worms in Mexico and roasted guinea pig in Peru. Grandma sparked my curiosity about things from outside of my own culture.

When Grandma died at eighty-nine, she still had most of her own teeth, and her wit was as sharp as ever. She claimed that she never had a headache in her whole life. She attributed it to her sugarless diet and black tea and coffee every day.

Excellent Dancer
Poland, 1930s

Grandma Maria loved to dance. She attended a number of parties organized by her husband's fellow army and navy officers. Among the officers she remembered best was Viktor Lomidze, of Georgian origin, later a naval commander during WWII.

One day she met another officer who invited her to a dance. The man was an excellent dancer. They danced several times and even tried the difficult foxtrot.

She later learned from somebody that the man had a wooden leg. This was well before the sophisticated prostheses available today.

Grandma frequently told this story as an example of how one can overcome various handicaps. Such stories encouraged me to overcome my own limitations. For example, I became a mountain climber in spite of my fear of heights. Now I'm writing this story in spite of my apparent dyslexia.

Grandma's Advice: Catching Crayfish

You leave after dark with a flashlight or a lantern. You approach the river or the lake and shine the light above the riverbank. A good place to hunt is where the riverbank is eroded with a deep niche under the bank where the crayfish may hide. As they come out toward the light, they can be caught by hand or with a net.

Like lobsters, you throw them alive in boiling water. This is not done out of gratuitous cruelty. As Grandma explained it to me, if they are still alive they will curl up their tail. If they don't, they were already dead and may not be fresh. Crustaceans go bad very quickly.

Years later I observed the same thing about blue crabs in Delaware: they come to the light. I also remembered Grandma's story when some people complained in the media about the practice of boiling lobsters alive. I knew from Grandma it was done to protect human health and possibly even life.

Psychic Phenomena
Poland, 1930s

Grandma was a practicing Catholic, and she went to confession the first Friday of every month. I remember her kneeling in a pew at St. John's Cathedral in Warsaw and crying. She said she was repenting for her sins.

But she also believed in reincarnation. It did not occur to me to ask her how she could believe in heaven or hell and, at the same time, in rebirth after death in another form. She probably did not give it much thought either.

She believed she had drowned in one of her previous lives, which explained why she was afraid of water. She never learned to swim. And there were only a few things she was afraid of. In her own words, she was as afraid of water as the devil is afraid of the holy water.

She was convinced that in another life she took part in the French revolution and saw Paris burning. This explained to her why her favorite color was red and why she liked fire so much. Her favorite flowers were red carnations.

As a young woman she went to visit a psychic recommended by a friend. He was an elderly gentleman with snow-white hair. He mentioned a lot of details from her life, things she thought he had no way of knowing. He also told her about her previous incarnations. He told her she could have two children, but she was not going to have any. It's hard to prove the former, but he was right about the latter.

Nevertheless, she helped raise three children she did not have: my mom, my sister, and me.

In the 1920s and 1930s, Grandma participated in a number of séances to communicate with the dead. She told me how they would make a plate marked with numbers and letters and make it spin by touching it with extended hands. She was told she was a good medium and that she could channel the spirits of the dead.

One day she was walking through the woods and she could hear music inside her head. When she got home she turned on the radio and heard the same music she had heard in the forest. This was well before portable radios. She was convinced she could receive radio waves.

Grandma's Joke: A Haunted House

There was this haunted house at the outskirts of some village. It was abandoned, with doors and windows long missing. People were afraid to walk by it as it was said evil spirits lived inside.

One brave villager decided to find out for himself. He approached the house and heard moans and groans emanating from inside. "What do you need, you poor soul?" he inquired.

"Do you have toilet paper?" was the reply.

WWII

I once picked up an American history textbook. The beginning of WWII was covered in one or two sentences. It sounded something like this: "Poland was conquered in less than a month. The Nazis employed the highly successful strategy of *blitzkrieg* (the lightning war)."

I'll try to elaborate a bit on this topic.

In 1938, Nazi Germany annexed Austria. The same year Germany, Poland, and Hungary, acting together, divided Czechoslovakia. Poland took a small enclave that, the Poles argued, was inhabited by ethnic Poles. The Czechs were not happy about being backstabbed by their fellow Slavic neighbors. Of course, it would not have happened if Czechoslovakia had not been betrayed first by her Western allies Britain and France, who signed the infamous treaty with Hitler in Munich.

By 1939, it was clear that Hitler was not going to leave Poland alone. Poland signed a treaty with Britain and France. If Poland was attacked, those two countries were obliged to immediately declare war on Germany and to come to Poland's rescue within fifteen days—the estimated time that the Polish army was prepared to resist the invasion.

On September 1, 1939 at 4:45 AM, German tanks rolled into Poland. At the same time, the German battleship *Schleswig-*

Holstein opened fire on the Polish Baltic Sea outpost Westerplatte. The 180 soldiers at Westerplatte were prepared to resist for twelve hours. They resisted for a week. They were falling asleep while shooting. When they finally took them prisoner, the Nazis let the commanding officer Major Sucharski keep his sword as a token of respect.

Another seminal battle of this campaign was the battle of Wizna, known as Polish Thermopylae. At Thermopylae, all Greeks died fighting the Persians. At Wizna, 720 Poles resisted 42,000 Nazis for three days. About eighty of them lived. The commanding officer, Captain Raginis, refused to surrender and blew himself up with a grenade in his bunker.

My Grandfather Jerzy (George), Grandma Maria's brother-in-law, fought in 1939, was taken prisoner, escaped, was captured again, and eventually ended up in a labor camp. After the war he received a medal for bravery.

The British waited three days to declare war on Germany. Initially, they accused the French of dragging their feet. Finally, they decided their honor was at stake as they made their pledge to Poland independently of France. But they did not do anything until after Poland was long occupied and after bombs were dropped on London. As Grandma Maria would put it, "They did not move a toe inside of a shoe" to help Poland. This period was known as the "phony war."

On September 17, the Soviets, allied with the Nazis, entered the eastern part of the Polish territory. The pretext was the same as Poles had when they took part of Czechoslovakia. The Soviets argued that they were protecting people culturally and linguistically linked to Mother Russia. They also recaptured the Belarusian territory taken by Poland after WWI.

Twenty-two thousand Polish officers and intellectuals were taken prisoner by the Soviets and eventually murdered in 1940. Most of them were taken to Katyń Forest by the NKVD, shot in the back of the head, and dumped into mass graves. Among them was my mother's godfather. When the Germans discovered the mass graves in 1943, the Western Allies quickly swept this inconvenient truth under the rug. They didn't want to upset the Soviets, now fighting on the same side.

I first heard the story of the Katyń massacre from Grandma Maria when it was still a taboo subject. We were walking back from my elementary school when I saw graffiti on the wall: "We shall avenge Katyń." Grandma explained what it meant.

Going back to WWII, Poland resisted the numerically and technologically superior Nazi and Soviet forces for a month, twice as long as it was expected to, longer than France did the following year. Then the government went into exile. Warsaw, where my grandparents lived with my three-year-old mother, suffered heavy casualties and fell after three weeks of siege. Grandma Maria was not with them at that time (I will get to that story later).

Poles quickly organized a resistance movement: secret armies in the cities and partisans in the countryside. One of the most prominent resistance organizations was the right-centrist Home Army led by the Polish government in exile in London. Grandma Maria became a soldier of the Home Army.

The occupation years in Warsaw were a period of brutal repression. The Nazis proceeded to exterminate the Jews, almost 30 percent of the city's population. They were crammed into the ghetto and slowly deported to death camps.

Non-Jewish Poles were denied education and used as slave labor. People were rounded up on the street and taken to labor camps in Germany.

After entering Cracow, the Nazis rounded up 144 professors and assistants of the Jagiellonian University, the second oldest in Central Europe after Prague, and deported them to Sachsenhausen concentration camp. The idea was to destroy the intellectual elite of the country and use the rest as cheap labor.

In 1940, under so-called AB Action (*Außerordentliche Befriedungsaktion*), 3,000 Polish intellectuals and well-known personalities were executed at Palmiry near Warsaw.

Polish resistance fighters organized underground education, blew up trains supplying the Eastern Front (Operation Wieniec), assassinated Nazi officials, and smuggled Jews out of the ghetto to provide them with fake papers (Żegota Committee). One of my mother's best friends, the late Jadzia, was one of the children smuggled out of the ghetto and placed with foster families. So was the former Polish foreign minister, the late Bronisław Geremek.

The punishment for hiding Jews was an automatic death sentence for all inhabitants of the building where the Jews stayed hidden.

For each killed German, the Nazis often executed 100 Poles picked at random. Walking today around Warsaw one encounters plaques saying: "Place sanctified by the blood of Poles. Here the 'Hitlerites' executed 100 Poles." The numbers differ. The plaques do not mention Germans or even the Nazis (technically, the members of NSDAP) but "Hitlerites" (followers of Hitler).

Most Warsaw citizens hated the occupiers and participated in or sympathized with the Resistance. A certain percentage that could claim some German ancestry became so-called *Volks-Deutche* (ethnic Germans). They were disliked by the Nazis who, according to Grandma, called them *Konjunktur Schweine* (opportunistic pigs). Poles considered them traitors.

The most despised group of Poles was the *szmalcowniks*, who blackmailed hiding Jews or Gentiles who helped them. The Home Army punished them with death.

All in all, during WWII, Poland lost six million people, about 17 percent of the population. This number includes about three million Polish Jews and three million others: intellectuals, resistance fighters, Catholic priests, the Roma people, and innocent civilians. Those were the highest relative casualties of any country (except perhaps Belarus, which was not independent before the war). For comparison, during the years the U.S. was involved in the war, more Americans died in automobile accidents than in the war itself. Of course, each war death is an individual tragedy.

Countries that are eager to send troops to other counties should remember the horrible effect of the war on the civilian population. For example, the U.S. has not experienced a war on its mainland territory since 1865, the end of the Civil War. It seems like the cycle of forgetting about the war is about fifteen to twenty years, about a generation. Then the saber rattling starts again.

After the war, Poland was not allowed to choose her own destiny. Churchill and Roosevelt and later Truman signed treaties with Stalin that left Poland in the Soviet area of influence. Churchill insisted on having democratic elections in postwar Poland, but he must have known how such elections would look like with the Soviet troops present. Poland felt betrayed by the West for the second time in five years.

Enter the Russians
Poland, 17 September 1939

Grandpa Johnny was assigned to the so-called Pińsk Flotilla. Grandma was in Pińsk (today's Belarus) when the Soviet Army invaded. First the airplanes appeared, dropping fliers. The message encouraged the Belorussians not to support the Poles.

Then the Soviet Army marched in. Grandma saw a column of Soviet soldiers greeted with traditional bread and salt by Jewish elders at the outskirts of Pińsk. "Under the Polish rule we had nothing," said one elderly Jew.

"*Teper' vsyo budet!* (Now you'll have everything!)," answered the Soviet officer at the head of the column.

Only a few years earlier Stalin's rule and collectivization of farms had brought starvation to the Ukraine, once known as the breadbasket of the Russian Empire.

On the other hand, the prewar Polish government wasn't always good to the Jews. In the 1930s they introduced a Jewish quota at the universities, limiting the number of applicants and made Jews sit separately from other students. Ironically, the

Nazis would soon limit educational opportunities for all Polish citizens.

Soon thereafter, Grandma was arrested by the NKVD (later known as the KGB). The NKVD officer who interrogated Grandma was tall, dark, impeccably dressed, and, in her own words, devilishly handsome. "Where is your husband?" he asked.

"What husband?" she replied with feigned surprise.

"Your husband, the navy officer you live with, go to restaurants with, drink with at the canteen!"

Grandpa Johnny had left town a few days earlier. Incidentally, Grandma retained her maiden name in all her documents. She did not anticipate this would happen. But she knew that, as a Polish officer's wife, she was in trouble. She knew some people who were taken to a Soviet camp never came back. She wondered where the Soviet officer got all his information.

She smiled seductively and answered in flawless Russian: "He is not my husband—he is my lover. I have no idea where he is."

"Is this right? You are free to go. Sorry for the misunderstanding," the handsome officer answered.

When she left the NKVD headquarters, she stopped smiling. Her knees were weak, her forehead covered with sweat. She went home to plan her return to Warsaw.

She had heard about the bombing of Warsaw. She had had no contact with her sister, Grandma Stefania, and my three-year-old mother. She made a vow that if she found them in good health, she would fast each Friday until the end of the war.

Upon returning to Warsaw she found out they were fine. She kept her vow and drank only water on Fridays until 1945.

Dangerous Food Ration
Warsaw, 1940s

Home Army private serial number 202, my Grandma, served as a courier carrying messages, weapons, and ammunition. One of her strategies was to mingle with the Germans. Warsaw trams were divided into two sections, very much like buses in the segregated South of the U.S. in the 1950s. The front section was *nur für Deutche* (only for Germans). The back section was for Poles. Before they were confined to the ghetto, Jews were not allowed on trams and sometimes even banned from sidewalks. My grandma, with her fluent and idiomatic German, would sit in the German section and shamelessly flirt with the Nazis. This protected her from random searches and roundups.

Once the Nazis stopped the tram, forced the Poles out, and put them in trucks bound for the railway station. They would end up in concentration and labor camps. Grandma watched the scene from the German section. She knew there was nothing she could do but survive and fight back.

With her dark brown hair and brown eyes, Grandma Maria did not look like a typical German, but she could get away with it. Her sister, Grandma Stefania, my mother's mother, was also dark, but with curly hair and deep-set brown eyes. Even though she was Catholic, she looked "Semitic" and was afraid she would be taken to a concentration camp as a Jew.

The Nazis did not always ask where one went to worship. They sometimes used anthropometric techniques to determine the "race." Somebody with a certain ratio of nose length to some other measurement could be in trouble.

Later, at the labor camp, Grandma Stefania was afraid they would take my blond mother away from her to be raised as a German. The joke in Warsaw at that time was: "What does a typical Aryan look like? Blond like Hitler, tall like Goebbels, slender like Goering." Hitler had dark hair, Goebbels was very short, and Goering was fat.

On another occasion, Grandma Maria was carrying a food ration (*Deputat*, an equivalent of 500-calorie-per-day diet as opposed to 2,400 calories recommended by the League of Nations at the time) in a big bag. On the bottom of the bag there was a 9-mm VIS automatic pistol with an extra clip. She also carried a smaller bag with her purse and other things.

She was stopped by a German soldier. *"Ausweis, bitte"* (Documents, please)," the German demanded.

Grandma smiled seductively and said: "I am sorry. I don't have a free hand. Could you hold this for me?" She gave him the bag with the gun inside and took out her ID from the other small bag.

The German looked into the big bag and saw potatoes, cabbage, and flour. *"Scheine Deputat!* (Nice ration)," he said. He gave her back the ID and said in French *"Bon appétit, madame!"* After he was gone Grandma leaned against the wall. Sweat was pouring down her face, and she almost fainted. She knew that if they found the gun, she would be first tortured and then probably killed.

One of her good friends, Janka, was taken to the notorious Pawiak prison where she was severely tortured. They had a special machine to drive needles under fingernails. It looked like a hollow metal imprint of a hand. According to Grandma's description from Janka's account, the device was electrified so that Janka's hand stuck to it and she could not pull out. Then five metal needles were simultaneously driven under her five fingernails. They also had another device specifically designed for beating the buttocks. They worked on Janka's buttocks until "pieces of flesh were flying through the air." She never told them anything.

Some conspirators, as Grandma recounted, were carrying cyanide at all times so that the Nazis would never take them alive.

Grandma's Advice: How to Survive a Poison Gas Attack

Grandma said that part of her military training as the Home Army soldier was to learn how to survive a poison gas attack. She said one was supposed to take out a handkerchief, pee on it, cover the mouth and nose, and breathe through it.

Even at that age I had an interest in chemistry and understood why water in urine could react with substances like chlorine or phosgene.

Hitler Speaking
Warsaw, 1940s

In Nazi-occupied Warsaw they would broadcast Hitler's speeches on the radio. Grandma Maria put her knowledge of German to use by listening to those speeches. She said that, even though she knew the man was a monster, even though she hated the Nazis, she was strangely drawn to his voice. She said the listener had a feeling he or she would like to follow that voice regardless of what Hitler was saying at the time.

This may give an insight as to why so many people did not oppose Hitler's ideas from the very beginning and followed him into the abyss, and some stayed with him to the end.

My mother and Grandma with muffs, Saxon Garden, Warsaw, 1943 or '44

Warsaw Uprising
Warsaw, 1944

By August 1944, the Soviet tanks were at the outskirts of Warsaw.

A year earlier the uprising in the Warsaw Ghetto took place. It was led by the ŻOB (Jewish Combat Organization), supplied with weapons and ammunition by the Home Army. It lasted three weeks. The 60,000 Jews remaining in the ghetto were not fighting to win; they were fighting to die with dignity. As one of the leaders, Marek Edelman, pointed out, they would not let the Nazis choose the time and place of their deaths. After the fall of the uprising, the Nazis destroyed the ghetto block by block and killed most of the insurgents.

On August 1, 1944, so called W hour (for Warsaw), a new uprising started. The Home Army, formally led by the Polish government in exile in London, wanted to liberate Warsaw and establish a Polish government before the Soviets moved in to establish Communist rule.

Grandma Maria was cut off from her battalion at the early stages of the Uprising and put in charge of civil defense of a group of buildings. She became a block commander. Her sister, Grandma Stefania, took care of my eight-year-old mother while hiding in the basement of one of the buildings. My mom told me how Grandma successfully coordinated the removal of incendiary bombs that fell on the building before they could cause any damage. It is possible that she saved the inhabitants' lives.

My mother recounts her eighth birthday there on August 15, 1944. She was half-starved. She got what she recalls to be the best gift of her life: a boiled potato. My mother still remembers the smell, taste, and texture of that potato. She also recalls asking her mother during a bombardment: "Do we all have to die now?"

One day a group of insurgents showed up at the building where Grandma Stefania was hiding with my mother. The group was led by a very young man, maybe eighteen. Grandma Stefania took my mom in her arms and said: "Look what you've done! Because of your stupid uprising, my little daughter is going to die!"

The young officer said to her: "For spreading defeatism you deserve a bullet in the head!"

Grandma Stefania's point was not entirely without justification. At that time the Nazi Germany was already losing the war. Some of the best, smartest, most talented, most patriotic Poles died in this heroic but ultimately futile gesture. A generation of educated Varsovians born around 1920 was almost entirely wiped out. America experienced a baby boom after WWII when the GIs returned home. In Poland there was a shortage of men.

Toward the end of the uprising, Grandma Maria's block was one of the few still standing on the street. It looked like a miracle, but Grandma was responsible for at least part of this miracle.

The uprising continued for sixty-three days, a full nine weeks. In the final stages, the insurgents used the city's sewers to escape the surrounded areas. All the while, the Soviets waited on the other side of the river Vistula. They waited for the Nazis to break Polish resistance. Then they moved in to "liberate" a pile of ruins.

Twenty thousand Home Army soldiers and two hundred thousand civilians died during the rising. The rest were taken prisoner. Grandma Stefania and my mother ended up at a camp in Pruszków and later at a labor camp in Rathenow, Germany. Grandpa Jerzy, captured earlier, was already in Germany working for a miller. Grandma Maria was first taken to a concentration camp.

After the Warsaw Uprising, 85 percent of the city lay in ruins. On Hitler's orders, the Nazis destroyed what remained of Warsaw. Again, they did it systematically, block by block, by using flamethrowers and explosives.

When Dwight Eisenhower, who saw devastated Berlin and Cologne, visited Warsaw right after the war, he said, "Warsaw is far more tragic than anything I've seen."

Mooing Cow
Warsaw, 1944

The Nebelwerfer was a six-barrel rocket launcher. It fired rockets over the period of ten seconds producing a loud screeching noise. Americans in the Sicily campaign called it "Screaming Mimi." Poles during the Warsaw Uprising called it "the mooing cow" or "the chest."

Home Army private serial number 202, my Grandma, was instructed to seek cover as soon as she heard the terrifying noise. If someone was caught on the upper floor of the building there was no time to go to the basement. The next best option was to stand under the outer wall. One day Grandma heard the piercing sound inside of a building and pressed herself against the wall, covering her head with her hands. Seconds later there was a terrifying explosion. When she turned around, half of the building, including the spot where she was standing before, was gone. It had turned into a smoking pile of rubble.

During the war, Grandma had several close brushes with death. They almost always involved decisions made by other people. In this case, the danger was anonymous and random, the same kind of danger most commonly faced by soldiers at the front line.

Rex
Warsaw, 1944

During the Warsaw Uprising food was scarce. Grandma saw young insurgents shoot pigeons and roast them on a split. She used to carry wheat grains in her pocket and chew them to cheat hunger.

Then one day she got an invitation for dinner. A couple she knew told her they managed to prepare a treat that included meat and potatoes. Grandma had almost forgotten what meat looked like. She was eager to come.

When she tried the meat at her friends' place, she did not like the taste of it. It tasted faintly sweet. Hungry as she was, she could not finish her portion. She apologized to her friends and suggested they give it to Rex. She was always fond of Rex, the spunky dog the couple owned. They told her it was regretfully impossible: the strange, sweet meat they were having for dinner *was* Rex.

Odd Number
Germany, 1944

After the Warsaw Uprising, Grandma was taken prisoner. A woman, possibly a traitor, was interviewing the POWs in flawless Polish. She asked Grandma about her age. Grandma lied and said that she was thirty-something while in fact she was forty-two. She did not know that this would save her life. Those over forty were considered unfit for hard labor and were liquidated.

Grandma boarded a cattle train. People were packed as tightly as sardines. There was no food or water. There was no bathroom. People did their business in one corner of the railroad car. After a while the stench was unbearable.

After a long and arduous journey she found herself at the notorious Ravensbrück women's concentration camp, ninety kilometers from Berlin. Between 1939 and 1945, over 130,000 female prisoners passed through the Ravensbrück camp system; only 40,000 survived. Therefore, the survival rate was about 30 percent. Although the inmates came from every country in German-occupied Europe, the largest single national group incarcerated in the camp consisted of Polish women. Among them was Maja Berezowska, one of Grandma's favorite artists.

Once in the camp, the prisoners were ordered to stand in a row. Grandma was standing next to her girlfriend. Naturally, they wanted to be close together. The Germans made them count off one-two, one-two. Ones, including Grandma, were taken to a dining hall and given soup, bread, and sausage.

Grandma had not seen such good food for a long time. "What are they up to?" she thought. "Are they going to fatten us first and then slaughter us like cattle?" She later learned that the twos, including her girlfriend, were taken to gas chambers and then to the crematorium. The Nazis did not have enough food and work for everyone, so they'd decided to leave each person's fate to chance.

Grandma was eventually taken to a Luftwaffe factory in Wittenau near Berlin.

When I mention to Americans that my grandma was, albeit briefly, taken to a concentration camp, I almost always hear the question: "Was she Jewish?"

Jews and the Roma people were, beyond doubt, the ones that suffered the most from the Nazis. But, as I mentioned before, about an equal number of non-Jewish Poles died during the war, many of them in the camps.

Labor Camp
Berlin, Wittenau, 1944–1945

"*Aufstehen*—get up!"

Each morning at 6 AM, the prisoners were awakened with this scream. They worked twelve-hour shifts. Dinner consisted of soup with a couple of unpeeled potatoes, with Swedish turnips thrown in. It was proudly called *Gemüse Sup* (vegetable soup). Coffee was made from roasted barley. French women ran the kitchen and received the best treatment from the Nazis because, as Grandma pointed out, unlike Poland, France surrendered. They allegedly retained the best food for themselves.

Russians were kept in a separate camp and were treated most harshly. Grandma remembers when a Russian man fell into a vat of acid used to clean metal sheets. He slowly perished while the guards and fellow prisoners looked on.

My memory of Grandma's story is a little hazy, but at some point she said she had to keep her bare feet in cold water used, I think, to quench the hot metal. She developed bunions and had them for the rest of her life. She said her eyelashes were silver from metal powder at the end of her shift.

Grandma was well liked by other prisoners and for her resourcefulness and courage gained the nickname, The Panther. One of her fellow prisoners even wrote a poem about her.

The original text written at Wittenau

Here is the translation:

Sunny, cheerful, smiling,
Loved by the boys, ladies, and girls,
Always calm, never gets angry,
Always well-rested, doesn't whine, doesn't yawn,
Pours elixir of life in our veins,
In one word—a loving, sincere, pleasant person,
Everyone treats her with respect,
She has beneficial influence on us,
Who are we talking about?—It's not hard to guess,
Because that's simply Maryna—The Panther!

Maryna is one of several variations of Maria. In her postwar documents her name was shown as Marianna (Maria Anna). She sometimes called herself Mańka.

Beautiful Hands
Berlin, Wittenau, 1945

On her first day at the Luftwaffe factory, Grandma was given a pair of cheap felt gloves without fingers. They were supposed to help workers carry hot sheets of steel from the furnace to the conveyor belt. "I am not going to wear those kraut gloves!" Grandma said to other women. She would grab the hot metal with her bare hands. The sheets were too heavy for her and too hot to handle, so she would use the top of her head to distribute the weight. After a few weeks she had a bald spot on top of her head. Forty years later she showed me the spot where the hair was still thinner.

Every few days an SS officer would come for inspection. He wore a black uniform with a black cap adorned with a dead man's skull. All the prisoners were scared of him. He had the power of life and death.

One day he came up to my grandma, watched her work for a while, and then suddenly asked: "Who are you?"

"*Ich bin eine banditin von Warschau*—I am a bandit from Warsaw," Grandma replied defiantly. This is how the Nazis referred to the insurgents. One person's freedom fighter is another person's bandit or terrorist.

"What am I doing?" she thought. "Now I am done for!"

"This is not what I am asking!" the SS officer replied sharply. "Are you married? Where is your husband?"

"He was a sailor. He sank with his ship," Grandma half-lied.

"*Schade, Schade*—pity, pity…" the German said and slowly walked away.

The next day Grandma received a package. It contained a pair of black leather gloves and a note. The note was written in Gothic script and said: "It would be a shame to waste such beautiful hands."

The SS later called her *Scheine schwartze Katze* (beautiful black cat).

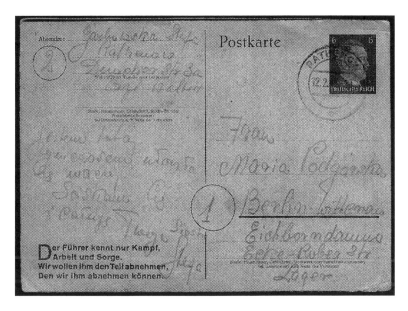

A letter from Grandma Stefania at Rathenow to Grandma Maria at Wittenau, 12 February 1945

Seventy Blows
Berlin, Wittenau, 1945

The penalty for each "offense" at a Luftwaffe factory in Wittenau was fifty "rubbers": blows with a heavy rubber club. Grandma was proud of committing three offenses at once.

Everyone was required to have a tag with a letter indicating nationality, in Grandma's case "P" for Polish. The tag was supposed to be stitched onto the jacket. Grandma had fake stitches on the outside of the tag and a safety pin underneath, which constituted offence number one.

The prisoners were allowed to leave the factory and go to town. They had to wear their clothes with tags on at all times. Grandma would put her tag with a safety pin in her pocket. With her fluent and idiomatic German she could pass for a native. This was offense number two.

The *Ausländers* (foreigners) were not allowed to enjoy entertainment reserved for the Germans, such as movies. Grandma would go to the movies. This was offense number three.

All along, Grandma knew the consequences. A woman was once caught on two offenses. They rounded up the prisoners, including Grandma, and made them watch the punishment. She was to receive one hundred blows from an SS guard. After the seventieth blow she stopped moaning. The SS noticed something was wrong and lowered his club to look a little closer. The woman was dead.

Grandma's "P" with fake stitches

Allons, Enfants …
Rathenow, 1945

Her sister Grandma Stefania, my actual grandmother, was at that time at another labor camp, Rathenow. She was no sissy either, even though she was responsible for my eight-year old mom. One day they brought French prisoners. Out of the blue, Grandma Stefania started singing: *"Allons, enfants de la Patrie, Le jour de gloire est arrivé!"*

The French prisoners looked at her and then continued the tune: *"Contre nous de la tyrannie …"*

German guards stood with their mouths open listening to *La Marseillaise* and did not know what to do. Fortunately, Grandma Stefania did not get into trouble.

Photo Receipt
Berlin, 1945

As I mentioned before, while working at a Luftwaffe factory near Berlin, Grandma would take a break from her twelve-hour shift and go into town. One day she decided to go to a photographer to have her photo taken so that she could send it to her family. The photographer gave her a receipt and told her to come back in a few days to collect the prints.

This was during the so-called carpet bombings of Berlin by the Allies. Grandma told me that first small airplanes would appear and throw pieces of aluminum foil to confuse German radars (at this stage of the war the Germans caught up with radar technology). Then squadrons of bombers would drop hundreds of bombs over a small area, turning entire neighborhoods into rubble.

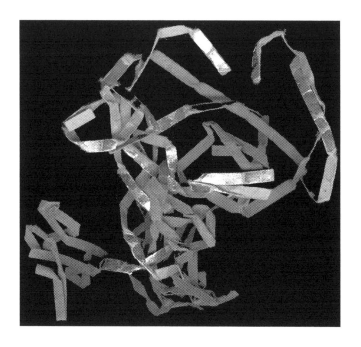

**Pieces of aluminum foil Grandma collected during the
bombing of Berlin**

A few days after her visit to the photographer, Grandma took
the receipt and went back to pick up the prints. At first she thought
she had lost her way. Then she checked the street name and
confirmed she was at the right place. Where the photographer's
shop once stood there was a flattened area extending over the
entire city block. There was not a stone left standing. White
dust covered everything. The destruction was so thorough that
Grandma said she could use the dust to powder her nose. She
wondered what had happened to the photographer but at the same
time remembered the near-total destruction of Warsaw only a few
months earlier. She felt both sad and elated.

More than thirty years later, Grandma showed me the photo
receipt and tiny strips of aluminum foil she had collected from
the street in Berlin.

A Good German
Berlin, 1945

With her *P* in her pocket, Grandma would go to Berlin, usually to see a movie. She mentioned places like Aleksanderplatz and Potsdamer Platz. The theaters were playing a lot of comedies, including American films with Charlie Chaplin and other comedians. Apparently, Chaplin's *The Great Dictator*, which made fun of Hitler himself, was forgotten.

She befriended a German woman who would invite her for dinner and, out of her meager ration, offered her food much better than at the camp. She took some of the food back to her fellow prisoners.

The German woman's husband was Polish, but he was not around; I don't remember what happened to him. Her son had joined the *Hitler Jugend* (Hitler Youth) as a boy and was now a thoroughly indoctrinated young SS officer. The woman was afraid that her own son would turn her in if he knew that she was helping a Polish prisoner of war. He had no scruples whatsoever. But she still risked being considered a traitor and continued helping Grandma.

The Pillory
Eastern Front, 1945

Toward the end of the war, Grandma was taken from the Luftwaffe factory near Berlin to the *Ost Front* (the Eastern Front) to dig trenches for the Nazis.

On her first day at the Eastern Front, Grandma was greeted by the gallows (Grandma consistently used the word *greeted* while retelling this story). There were four men swinging from the beam. She was told that they were traitors and cowards.

German women, wives and daughters of local farmers, were ordered to lock up all the wells. They secured them with chains and padlocks so that the prisoners digging trenches were forced to drink from ditches. Grandma recalls drinking from a ditch full of tadpoles.

In the middle of one of the villages there was a pillory. Tied to it was a German woman. She was stripped naked and put inside a potato sack so that only her head was sticking out. Her head was shaved. Her face was full of cuts and bruises. German soldiers passing by were spitting at her, throwing stones and chunks of dried mud. The woman was accused of helping the prisoners.

The Liberators
Germany, 1945

Grandma was digging trenches for the Germans while the Soviets were approaching from the east. She could hear their cannons closer and closer every day.

One day she woke up in the morning, and the Germans guards were gone. In fact, everyone was gone. She took a walk through the abandoned village. Around the corner she saw a man. She later told me he looked like a monkey: long trunk and short, bowed legs of a chimpanzee, long hands, unshaven face, flat nose, and big ears. He had a red star on his cap. A Belgian Nagan revolver, Soviet Army issue, was hanging low on his hip. She could smell alcohol on his breath.

He pulled out his gun and pointed at the door of the nearby barn. They walked inside. "*Krasavitza* (Beauty)!" the man said. "*Budesh moya* (You will be mine)!"

"*Ne budu* (I won't be)," replied Grandma resolutely. She was up against the wall with no room to move.

Scared as she was, she could not help thinking that "*krasavitza*" was not quite the right expression. Her stomach was bloated from hunger, her hair in disarray. She said that, after she combed her hair, her comb would walk away on the backs of lice.

The first bullet lodged itself in the barn wall next to her right cheek, sending splinters of wood. The next one went a little higher. A couple more went above her head. The man paused and repeated his request. Grandma said no one more time. Pretty soon her head was surrounded with bullet holes that formed something of a halo. She reminisced later that, despite what he did to her, the guy deserved the top grade for marksmanship.

Suddenly, she heard steps outside. "*Komandir idet* (Officer in charge is coming)," Grandma said. The soldier put away his gun and left the barn in a hurry. Grandma leaned against the wall. Her resistance almost cost her life.

Some hours later she looked at her reflection in the mirror. The dark hair on her temples had turned white. Eventually it returned to the original color.

Swimming Lesson
WWII

Grandma recalled a story of a female friend who, like herself, could not swim. At some point she was running away from the Nazis. I do not remember if she escaped from a camp or if this was some other situation where she would have been killed if she got caught.

The only escape route was across a deep river. She walked into water with her eyes fixed on the other bank. She did not recall how she did it, but she found herself on the other side, exhausted but safe.

Moderation
Poland, 1945

After the liberation, Grandma was seriously undernourished. She received her first full meal in months. Some of the other former prisoners wolfed up the food. A lot of them became violently ill. Their stomachs had shrunk and were unprepared to receive so much food. Grandma heard stories of people dying from overeating.

Grandma controlled her hunger and ate slowly in small portions. Eventually, her bloated stomach disappeared, and she was once again her normal self.

Tainted Wine
Pomerania, Poland, 1945

After the war ended, Grandma found herself in the western part of Poland, which had belonged to Germany before the war. With a group of people, she entered an abandoned estate with a wine cellar. Inside the cellar was a huge oak barrel of wine with a tap on the side. One of the men opened the tap. Red liquid started pouring onto the floor. Somebody found a couple of glasses. A libation soon followed. "Great wine," one of the men commented. "Must have been here for several months. Come on, have some," he said to Grandma.

For some reason, Grandma was in no mood for drinking. At some point the wine stopped flowing. One of the men climbed the ladder to reach the top of the barrel and opened the lid. He looked inside, his face turned pale, and he almost fell off the ladder. Inside the barrel there were three or four corpses wearing German uniforms. The barrel was still half-full but one of the corpses must have floated toward the tap and his body blocked the orifice.

All the men who had partaken became violently sick and started throwing up. Grandma thanked God she was not tempted. Her poison was always clear vodka.

Grandma's Joke: Puking Drunk

A drunk threw up on the street. A dog came by and started licking the puke. The drunk looks on the ground, looks at the dog, and says: "I remember the tomatoes; I remember the green peas. But I c-can't remember the dog!"

Faithful Dog
Warsaw, 1944–1945

Grandma had a villa in a village of Świdry Małe near Warsaw. She used to go there to escape the German-occupied city. There, the caretakers looked after her favorite dog, Urwis ("Rascal"). She could not keep him in the city. Besides, keeping the dog in the starving city would be frivolous. In the countryside it was easier to find leftover food for the mutt.

Rascal loved Grandma. He would almost jump out of his skin when he saw her. They could play for hours. He would accompany her everywhere. Grandma said he always knew she was coming even though she was still on the train and miles away. He seemed to have a sixth sense.

Grandpa Johnny with dogs. One of them could be Rascal.

During the Warsaw Uprising, Grandma could not leave the city. Then she was taken prisoner. Almost a year later, after the war ended, she briefly returned to Warsaw. There was no Warsaw. Only a pile of ruins remained.

She went to Świdry Małe. The villa was abandoned. There was no one around. The once meticulously maintained garden was now overgrown with weeds. She sat down on a porch.

Suddenly she saw something move in the bushes. It was Rascal. He half-walked, half-crawled toward her. He could not bark, he could not even wag his tail, but his eyes were full of joy. She picked him up and put him on her knees. He rested his head on her lap. Minutes later he was dead.

Grandma had no idea how he had survived so long without food. Apparently he was waiting for her for months and died happy, knowing that she had not abandoned him like everyone else.

Hare Hunt
Pomerania, Poland, 1940s

After the war, Poland gained part of the formerly German territory. Because of her background in economics and her membership in the Socialist Party before WWII, Grandma became president of a bank in a small town in Pomerania. She was assigned a limousine with a chauffeur. In her own words, she was "on top of the candlestick."

Working Woman, undated

Communist rule brought oppression, lack of basic freedoms, and relative poverty. However, one positive thing it did was to open opportunities for women which were unthinkable before the war. Like a steamroller, it flattened old traditions, including the tradition of male domination in the economy and leadership. Women rode tractors, shoveled coal, and, yes, ran banks.

About that time Grandpa Johnny resurfaced. He said he spent the war fighting as a partisan. As far as Grandma knew, he had mostly been making moonshine. At this point he was drinking heavily. He begged Grandma to go back to him. She refused. Eventually, they divorced.

Grandma often visited branches of her bank in the countryside. She made sure no money was missing and provided employee training. Coming back home late at night, Grandma and her chauffeur would drive through fields and meadows.

Her chauffeur developed a unique way of hunting hares. On a road with no traffic he would turn off the headlights. There were many hares in the area. They got spooked by the noise. At least one would get hit by the oncoming car while running blindly across the road. They collected the bounty, took it home, and fixed it. Grandma always said the hare's meat smelled of wind (meaning it had a gamey taste). The best part was the rear. The meat was excellent to make pâté. Although I had rabbit many times, I had to wait a long time to try hare pâté. It is really good.

Going to Church
Pomerania, Poland, 1940s

Grandma became a member of the Polish United Workers Party, a Soviet-model totalitarian Socialist Party, without ever joining. She was a lifelong Socialist and a member of the Socialist party before WWII. After the war, under Soviet supervision, The Polish Socialist Party united with the Communist Polish Workers Party to form the Polish United Workers Party.

Poland was never de facto fully Communist. Most of the land remained in private hands. Limited private enterprise was permitted. Stalin himself admitted that trying to establish Communism in Poland was like trying to saddle a cow.

After the war, many of her Home Army friends ended up in prison, some of them with death sentences. The party did not know about Grandma's former affiliations. It also did not know that she went to church every Sunday, something a good Communist was not supposed to do.

During one of the party meetings, the chairman said: "Comrade such-and-such told us that comrade Maria goes to church. Is this true, comrade Maria?"

"Yes, it's true. But how does comrade such-and-such know about it? I'll tell you how. Comrade such-and-such also goes to the church. He enters though the side door. I enter through the main entrance! Don't we have freedom of worship in this country?" Comrade such-and-such was kicked out of the party. Grandma stayed.

In her role as a party member, she was on first-name terms with the dreaded head of state security in the small town of Stargard in Pomerania. One day they captured a farmer accused of supporting the Home Army which, after Germany's surrender, still waged partisan war against the Communists. The farmer faced a stiff prison sentence, if not worse.

Grandma went to talk with the head of security. "Listen, Tadek," she said. "This poor peasant knows nothing about politics. He is used to soldiers coming and taking what they want. The Nazis did it, now the partisans do it. Why don't you let him go?" They let him go.

One of Grandma's Home Army friends recalled that during the war he was arrested and tortured by the Gestapo. After the war he was arrested by the Polish state security. Afterwards, he said that the Germans treated him better.

Grandma used to say that Poland was Socialist; the Soviet Union was Communist. "We are not there yet." Even as a schoolboy I could detect irony in her voice. She always hated the Soviet domination. But she did what it took to remain influential in rebuilding Poland after WWII. She got a Pomeranian Griffon medal for her efforts.

In 1980, now retired, Grandma joined the free Solidarity Trade Union.

Grandma's Joke: Going to the Soviet Union

A man was crossing the border between Poland and the Soviet Union. The Soviet border guard asked him: "What's your name?"

"Sirloin," the man replied.

"We have no 'sirs' here," the guard replied. He added, to the person taking notes, "Write down: Comrade Loin."

Drunken Pigs Pomerania, Poland, 1940s

A lot of farmers at that time were making moonshine to supplement their income. The government had the monopoly on making liquor, and police raids were frequent.

Grandma visited a moonshiner to try his product. She knew the taste well from the time of the Nazi occupation. It reminded her of cognac, which is why she was never too crazy about cognac. She preferred unflavored vodka.

Anyway, the moonshiner was tipped off that the police were on their way. He poured the moonshine into the pond in the middle of his farm's courtyard and hid the still in the bushes.

The pigs and ducks enjoyed the muddy pond. The animals would drink from it, swim on it, and take mud baths.

When the police arrived, they were greeted by a huge hog. He was staggering from side to side under his considerable weight. Finally, he fell and could not get up. The ducks looked even more interesting. Never known for steady gait, they were now running in zigzags and circles. Grandma never saw anything like it.

She knew pigs liked alcohol. They shared a lot with people, including omnivorous eating habits, high intelligence, and lack of moderation. The ducks were more of a surprise.

Grandma's Joke: Going to America

Comrade Rozenblum worked for a state factory in Warsaw. He was in charge of selling the product.

He was sent to sell some of the product to the brotherly nation of Czechoslovakia. He telegraphed back: "Product sold. Long live free Czechoslovakia."

Next he was sent to Hungary. He telegraphed back: "Product sold. Long live free Hungary."

For his dedication he was sent to the United States of America to earn some hard currency. He telegraphed back: "Product sold. Money collected. Long live free Rozenblum."

Pet Chickens
Pomerania, Poland, 1950s

For a while, Grandma kept two pet chickens. One of them was a miniature "Lilliput" hen, as Grandma described her. The other one was also a hen that laid an egg a day. I found it hard to believe, but I verified in the literature that certain breeds can produce over 300 eggs a year.

Grandma immensely enjoyed her two feathery companions. I am not sure where she kept them because, to my knowledge, she lived in the city and did not have a courtyard or a garden. I never had a chance to ask her.

My Mother
Warsaw, 1953

Eventually, Grandma Maria moved back to Warsaw. Having no children of her own she spent a lot of time with my mother. She was a real doting aunt. She took Mom to the movies, for walks in a park, to the beach.

Grandma's defiance—all the stories she told about how she stood up to the Nazis and the Soviets—influenced my mother when she was a teenager. When my mother was a high school student in the early 1950s, she was one of the only two students in her class who were not members of the Communist youth organization ZMP (Association of Polish Youth).

When Stalin died in 1953, a lot of members of the Association of Polish Youth looked distraught and sad. Some girls had red eyes, some cried. When Mom saw their faces, she burst out laughing. She rejoiced that the monster was finally dead.

My mother and Grandma

This cost her admission to the medical academy. Even though she passed the entrance exam, the Association of Polish Youth members wrote a negative opinion about her, which resulted in a rejection letter from the academy. "We have no room for you," the letter said.

Instead, she applied to Warsaw University and eventually got her PhD in chemistry.

Eels and Carp
Poland, 1970s

Smoked eel was one of Grandma's favorite dishes until the day she saw the corpse of a drowned person pulled from the sea in Pomerania. The corpse was swollen and covered with seaweed. In Grandma's own words, "Small eels were coming out of all the body orifices." They were wriggling like snakes. From then on Grandma stopped eating eel.

But she still loved carp. We would buy live carp for Christmas and keep them in a bathtub for a few days to make sure they were fresh. Nobody had the heart to kill them. At that point they were like pets.

Then Grandma Maria was summoned. She put salt behind their gills to "ease their suffering," grabbed them by the tail one by one, and hit their heads against the edge of the sink a few times until the blood was on the wall. Then she would take a knife, disembowel them, and cut off their heads. Soon, they were on a plate.

Grandma's Advice: Rat Trap

Fill a barrel half-full of water, and leave it for the night at a place frequented by rats. Cover the top of the barrel with thick paper secured by a piece of string. Make two intersecting cuts in the paper. Lean a wooden board against the edge of the barrel. Leave some seeds or other food under the barrel, on the board, and on the paper.

Rats climb to the top of the barrel and fall through the hole in the paper. Those already trapped inside make noise and seem to encourage others to join them. In the morning the barrel will be full of drowned and half-drowned rats!

Inspired by this story, I built several mousetraps. I was eight or nine at the time. None of my traps worked. Eventually, I would become a real inventor.

I recently saw the description of "Grandma's" rat trap in a book about invention.

Grandma and I
Warsaw, circa 1972

I am six years old. I am playing with my Grandma Maria, who is seventy. Our one-bedroom apartment is different from others. There are two doors leading from the kitchen to the living room. The kitchen is divided by a cabinet to form another small room with a picture of a nude woman in the middle of the meadow by Renoir and two realistically rendered lovers by Picasso.

One can make a circle walking between the three spaces. Grandma is stalking me. This is the game she invented. She calls it "Bambi-bambi-bambino."

Every now and then she changes direction and approaches me from the other side. I have to be on my toes and look in both directions if I don't want to be surprised by Grandma sneaking behind me and screaming in my ear "Bambi-bambi-bambino!"

I best remember Grandma Maria as a woman in her mid-seventies and early eighties, slightly overweight but fit (my mom said Grandma was never exactly thin), elegantly dressed, her dark graying hair forming a halo around her head, her brown eyes radiating warmth. She was flashing her own teeth in a ready smile (many people of her generation wore dentures at this age), commenting on current events, telling jokes, sometimes swearing "Cholera!" or "Dog's blood!"

Grandma Maria lived in a tiny one-bedroom apartment in the Warsaw borough of Wola with her sister Grandma Stefania and Grandpa Jerzy. She occupied a tiny bedroom while they shared the living room. The apartment was from the 1950s, and so was the furniture, with cut-glass lighting fixtures and a black-and-white TV set that had a glowing point in the middle of the screen after it was turned off. In the living room hung a painting of *Sower with Setting Sun* by Van Gogh and *Storks* by Chełmoński, which represented a typical mix of Polish and world's culture my family taught me to appreciate. I will describe Grandma's room later.

On the weekend we would take a tram to visit the grandparents. We could watch TV there. We did not buy a TV set until I was eight and my mom was thirty-eight. My grandparents' house had an old elevator and a garbage chute. The staircase always smelled slightly of rotting garbage.

Grandpa Jerzy (George) died in 1974 at the age of 64. I was eight at the time. He was strong and athletic, but he drank and smoked too much. He was smart and very knowledgeable but did not have the motivation to finish college. His various occupations included lifeguard at a resort, civil servant, miller, and pig farmer. He taught me about stars, meteors, koalas, and panda bears.

He was a keen practical joker. Once he hit me in the head with a chestnut and told me it was a meteor. Another time he told me I could see the stars through the sleeve of his jacket. When I looked through it he poured a cup of water through the sleeve right in my face. He taught me to play a "guitar" on my nose. He showed me how to float motionless down the river facedown. He called it the "corpse stroke." He showed me how to make a carbonated drink from vinegar and baking soda. When I asked him about his dentures, he said it was a horse's jaw. I concluded he did not need a horse's jaw, so I threw them through the window. One day he let me smell fresh-ground horseradish. It was so painful I started hitting him with my small fists.

Grandma Stefania was also funny but in her later years more worried about everything. She was a good cook. She made my favorite dish of mashed potatoes mixed with flour and fried with bacon cracklings. Despite her type two diabetes, she smoked and ate sweets. I remember her smoking while cooking, ash dropping on the food. She was very different from her sister, Grandma Maria, who hated smoking and tried unsuccessfully to make her quit. "Get rid of that chimney!" Grandma Maria would say.

Despite having completed only ten grades, Grandma Stefania worked as an accountant in an office. In the 1970s she still used an abacus. I was impressed that she dealt with numbers of the order of billions or even trillions.

I lived with my parents in a different part of the city, in Warsaw's Old Town, now UNESCO's World Heritage Site. Eventually a family of four, we occupied a one-bedroom apartment. The house was originally a seventeenth-century granary. It was mostly destroyed during WWII and rebuilt in the same style.

The house is still standing on an escarpment overlooking the river Vistula, and my family still lives there. The roof is slated and covered with red shingles. The house is connected to the Old Town by a bridge. This is the only house with a bridge I ever saw, except for the medieval castles like the castle in Segovia, Spain. The house is located within a five-minute walk from the Royal Castle and St. John's Cathedral.

The apartment is full of books, as it was then. Two walls are completely covered with bookshelves, well over two thousand titles in five or more languages.

Grandma's Dogs and Horses
Warsaw, 1970s

As I mentioned before, Grandma loved animals, especially dogs and horses.

In Poland in the seventies there were only two TV channels. We could only receive one of the channels.

There was a movie theater in Warsaw that showed old movies. Grandma took me to see *Old Yeller* and *Lady and the Tramp*. This was quite a treat compared to the tiny, grainy black-and-white screen. I do not remember much of *Old Yeller* except the sad ending that upset me. I vividly remembered the scene from *Lady and the Tramp* when the dogs rescue Lady from the dog catcher. I recently saw the cartoon again. I found it a little too syrupy.

Watching TV shows about horses was a ritual Grandma and I shared. There were two of them: the Polish show *Karino* and the British *Adventures of Black Beauty*. *Karino* was about a racehorse that broke his leg. They almost euthanized him, but a young woman fought for his life. Eventually, he recovered and raced again.

Black Beauty was about a girl and a boy who adopt an unusually smart black horse. Together they share many adventures that often involve crime and danger. Somehow, the horse is the center of each of episodes. I recently bought it on DVD and watched it for the first time since I saw it with Grandma as a child.

Grandma bought me several books about animals, including a collection of dog stories, another one about cats, and a third one about horses, all by the same author. She also bought me *Rascal* by Sterling North, an American story about a pet raccoon. Our favorite book, mine and Grandma's, was *The Wind in the Willows* by Kenneth Grahame featuring our favorite character: Mr. Toad.

Grandma also loved shows that didn't involve animals, namely the *Columbo* and *Kojak* mystery series. "Such a handsome baldy," she often said of Kojak.

Gander
Poland, 1970s

Urle was a sleepy village. I spent my summer vacations there when I was in kindergarten and the first grade. The streets were adorned with yellow and orange marigolds. The local store near the train station smelled of cheap carbonated orange soda that contained no real orange juice. It was at that store that I learned to drink from a bottle. Grandma Maria taught me not to suck the neck of the bottle but to leave an opening to let the air in.

One day Grandma and I were walking to the bakery to buy bread. I liked going to the bakery. I liked the smell of fresh-baked bread, and I liked to watch the bakers put white dough in the oven with special wooden shovels and pull out golden brown loaves. Now I make my own bread.

On our way to the bakery, we would pass a horse-powered wheel used to grind grain. Near the wheel we came across a flock of white geese. I approached them too closely and was attacked by a gander. The bird chased me, flapping his wings and hissing like a snake. Grandma hit him over the head with her shopping bag, and he ran away. To a six-year-old, this was quite an adventure. Grandma was very proud of her fight with the gander. "I showed him!" she would say.

Grandma and I used to visit a Russian woman named Nadia who lived nearby. Nadia would give me something to eat, and she and Grandma would speak Russian. As I found out later, she had no reason to like the Russians, but she was friendly to anyone who was friendly to her.

Another person taking care of me in Urle was my nanny, a superstitious village woman also named Maria. She told me that hell, full of devils and the accursed, was located underground. She also told me that when one hears ringing in the ear, it is an angel chasing away the devil with a tiny bell. She lit candles during thunderstorms. She told me Jesus was crucified with only three nails because the fourth one was stolen by a Gypsy. Grandma Maria had to set me straight.

One day Grandma found me digging a hole in the courtyard with my tiny shovel. "What are you doing?" she asked.

"I'm digging a hole to reach hell and see the devil!" I replied.

Polish Lesson
Poland, 1970s

I was maybe five or six years old. I had just learned to write in capital letters. Grandma was helping me out. I wrote my name: "ADAM." Then I wrote "*DUPA*" which is a vulgar expression for buttocks in Polish. Finally, I wrote "*GUWNO*" (shit). Grandma was not pleased. "This is not how you spell it," she said. "It should be *gówno*; 'u' and 'ó' are pronounced the same way." And she smiled.

Grandma's matter-of-fact approach prevented me from becoming too fascinated with swear words like some of my childhood friends. To me they were just words used in certain situations.

Grandma's Treasure Chest
Warsaw, 1970s

As I said before, we used to visit Grandmas Stefania and Maria on Sundays. They lived together in a small apartment they had shared with Grandpa Jerzy until his death in 1974. I would retreat to Grandma Maria's tiny room and ask her about the history of objects she owned.

She had a sizeable "treasure" chest full of various odds and ends, mostly objects from WWII. It included letters, strips of aluminum foil that the Allies dropped on Berlin to jam the radar before carpet bombings, her mother's seal with her coat of arms (a hawk), a block of sealing wax, photographs, old imperial rubles, a pre-WWII token from a casino (there were no casinos in Socialist Poland), a horseshoe magnet, opera binoculars, a magnifying glass, an oriental fan, and more.

One of the war letters contained my mother's drawing. In her childish style, all circles, she depicted the entire family as cats.

One of the postcards was a German propaganda drawing depicting women in overalls working in an airplane factory with the caption, "Women are working for us." They were like Rosie the Riveter, only on the opposite side. I regret Grandma giving it to me because I lost it.

I also lost the imperial rubles with the image of Empress Catherine the Great and the watermark. As soon as I learned some Russian I deciphered that they could have been exchanged for pure gold, of course before 1917.

Grandma also showed me how to use the sealing wax. She melted it over the candle and sealed a letter with Great-Grandma's seal.

She told me the story of the gaming token. She said she used to go to casinos a lot. As I said before, she taught me to play war, poker, and blackjack. She also taught me a couple of solitaires. I remember one involved uncovering as many cards as possible; the other one produced sets of four jacks, queens, etc. Those groupings could be used to foretell the future.

In addition to the poem written in her honor by a fellow prisoner at the Luftwaffe factory, Grandma's treasure chest also contained other poems written by fellow prisoners. The rhymes were awkward, but the emotion was unmistakable.

On the wall at Grandma's room hung a painting of a nun. It had once belonged to a German family living in Eastern Pomerania before and during WWII. They were forced to flee after the war. The Germans were uprooted from the area where they had lived, sometimes for centuries, while the Poles were forcefully removed from the eastern part of the pre-war Polish state that became part of the Soviet Union.

Being in a position of power and prominence in Pomerania, she could have become rich acquiring the property of displaced people. She only took the few items that were given to her with her apartment and now fit into this tiny room.

As I mentioned before, Grandma's father lost his fortune after WWI. Then Grandma lost everything again during WWII. This is part of the reason why my family valued education, knowledge, and tradition much more than any material possessions that could easily be taken away. This is what my mother and I learned from Grandma. Mom was often full of contempt for the "bourgeois," who were preoccupied with money and status.

Grandma also had a wooden statue of an elephant with real ivory tusks. She rescued it from a burning house. The statue, burnt on one side, now belongs to my sister. I pulled out and lost one of the tusks. Years later I saw an almost identical wooden elephant in Thailand, and I remembered Grandma.

Next to the elephant stood a small radio and a lamp with a bronze sculpture of a wild boar under a tree. The light bulb was on top of the tree. The boar looked very lifelike. Next to the lamp was a small bronze sculpture of a bear sitting on a real stone.

A painted Chinese vase stood next to the bear. According to an expert, it was a German forgery, a very good one. The paintings depicted children at play. Grandma also had a Japanese doll. She dressed her in clothes she made herself. She also made her own muffs from the fur she purchased.

Asking Grandma about different items usually started a new topic of conversation. When I asked about the Chinese vase, she would tell me about the foot-binding practice in China, the swallow nest soup, or dinner at the Chinese Embassy, things she had heard about, read about, or experienced herself.

Above the door hung a horseshoe with the inscription "Baltimore, MD," a gift from friends from America, "for good luck" as Grandma put it. Somehow, I thought Baltimore had something to do with the Baltic Sea. It would be years before I went there and tried the crab cakes.

Grandma always had a pile of monthly magazines, similar to *Reader's Digest*, with reprints of articles from the world's press. They kept her up to date with current events. She also had a book on Greek myths I liked to browse through.

Occasionally, Grandma would pull out her old cream-colored gramophone and a collection of vinyl records. I would ask her to play "The Ducky" or "Monika." "The Ducky" was a song, I think originally Italian, about a little duck who tragically falls in love with a poppy flower. I was always moved by the ending. The duck goes to the meadow to look for her poppy flower and finds out the meadow was cut. "Monika" was about a little girl who liked to skate. I had a friend named Monika, and I liked the song.

Grandma would play a lottery every week and ask me to help her pick the numbers. This reminded her of her old gambling days. Watching the numbered lottery balls spin on TV gave her a thrill.

My First Camera
Warsaw, 1974

Grandma bought me a camera for my first communion when I was eight. It was called Ami, and it used film wider than 35 mm.

I immediately went to the sandpit to take pictures of the "desert"—sand formations up close. None of them came out. Years later I would take much better desert pictures on Wadi Rum in Jordan and on the Sahara in Morocco.

I'm now on my eighth camera. Grandma was the one who got me interested in photography. She always promised to buy me a microscope to "see a drop of water," but they were expensive and hard to come by.

With Grandma on the day of my First Communion, Warsaw, May 1974

Burning Christmas Tree
Warsaw, 1970s

One Christmas, as always, my parents and I visited the grandparents in their apartment. Grandma Maria would buy a small Christmas tree each year and decorate it herself. That year she bought sparklers and put them on the tree next to the ornaments.

Grandma and I were alone in her room when she lit a couple of sparklers. A shower of bluish sparks surrounded the green tree.

Then the tree caught fire. The wire of one of the sparklers had gotten so hot that it was glowing red.

In her mid-seventies, Grandma displayed the same composure and quick wit that had saved her skin more than thirty years earlier during WWII. She threw the burning tree on the floor and rolled up the carpet, wrapping the tree inside and smothering the flames.

This little adventure became one of my fondest Christmas memories.

Grandma's Anecdote: Prince Radziwill Panie Kochanku

Radziwill Panie Kochanku, the eighteenth-century Polish-Lithuanian prince, was known for his sense of humor and his idiosyncrasies. (*Panie Kochanku* means "My Dear Sir" in Polish; this was his favorite expression.)

One day Prince Radziwill threw one of his usual lavish parties. He invited a certain nobleman known for his wit. Soup was served. All the guests got a spoon, except this one nobleman. "You're a fool if you don't eat the soup," said the prince to everybody.

The nobleman cut a heel of bread, removed the soft part, and proceeded to eat his soup with the heel. When he was done, he said: "You're a fool if you don't eat your spoon!"

Little Black
Warsaw, 1970s

Grandma would pick me up at the elementary school and walk me home. In winter she kept her hands in a muff where she kept all her belongings. She was probably the only person in Warsaw still carrying a muff.

We walked across the New Town, passing Marie Curie's Museum in a house where she was born. Soon we would reach the Old Town, the UNESCO's World Heritage site meticulously restored after WWII.

On our way home we passed the Barbican, the old city gate made from red brick. There was a soda fountain on wheels in front of the gate. Grandma would buy me soda with raspberry juice in a poorly washed glass everyone drank from.

Inside the Barbican an old woman was selling toy animals made from rubber. Grandma bought me a different animal each time: a mouse, a bat, a frog. I had quite a collection. Then we would buy some heart-shaped gingerbread and head to the Krokodyl (Crocodile) coffee shop for Grandma's "little black"—a small cup of black coffee.

Grandma had low blood pressure, and coffee kept her going. She used to enjoy visiting the mountain resort of Zakopane. She asked her doctor if it she could still go there. The doctor said she could, but, in his own words, she should be aware that, because of the altitude, she might end up at a local cemetery.

Sometimes my friend Monika would join us on our way home and at the Crocodile. Grandma would buy us a cola, a WZ cake with chocolate and whipped cream (a Warsaw specialty from 1950s), or a hamburger. This was the only place in Warsaw where one could buy hamburgers. Grandma had limited resources but did not mind treating us. Over the meal she would tell us one of her stories.

After we got home, Grandma would often help me with my homework. Learning was a family affair. Both Grandma and Mom helped out and offered suggestions.

Grandma often said my handwriting was like chicken scratches under a fence. I also often heard that I was certifiably lazy. She used to say: "If you want to do well in school, you have to sit down on your ass and study!"

When I was younger she would read me books. I would take advantage of it even though I could read well. While reading *The*

Three Musketeers she would explain how to pronounce French names. I think she read me my first mystery novel, *The Hound of the Baskervilles*, when I was eight. At that time I almost abandoned children's literature and devoured more mystery novels.

In the evening Grandma would take a tram back to her apartment.

Grandma's Puzzle
1970

"Answer this," said Grandma when I was maybe nine. "On the Polish–Czech border a rooster laid an egg. To which country did the egg belong?"

I thought hard. Maybe they should cut the egg in half so that the two halves could be shared by the two countries? Maybe they should flip a coin?

"Rooster!" said Grandma. "Rooster!" she repeated. I was still in the dark.

Finally she explained, "Roosters don't lay eggs!"

German Lesson
Poland, 1970s

Here is a poem Grandma told me to help me remember a few words in German:

"A hat is *Mütze*.
Buckwheat is *Grütze*.
Bacon is *Speck*.
Shit is *Dreck*."

Sometimes she would also speak to me in French: *"Enfant gâté!"* Or she would sing a lullaby in Russian: *"Spi mladenets, moi prekrasny …"*

She also taught me the basics of German and French spelling. Her English was limited to "All right" and "Whisky and soda."

Thanks to Grandma, my early exposure to different languages sparked my interests in linguistics and made me study five languages in addition to my native Polish (although I still did not have a choice when it came to Russian—a requirement in Poland at that time).

It did not hurt that my paternal Grandmother Janina was a poet, writer, linguist, and translator published in several languages. She had a degree in Polish and Romance languages and translated Sappho from the ancient Greek. She also studied differential equations just for fun.

Sometimes, when Grandma Maria picked me up after school, we would take bus number 125 from New Town's Square to Grandma Janina's apartment on the other side of town. The women talked for hours while I immersed myself in Grandma Janina's book collection or played with snails in her garden.

How I "Saved" Grandma
Krynica, Poland, 1970s

Grandma and I in Krynica

Grandma and I spent several vacations together, just the two of us. We went twice to the mountain spa of Krynica Górska, to Polanica (another spa), and to a number of other places.

My fondest memories are from Krynica. Grandma was a big spa fan. She bought us special cups to drink mineral water. They had a goose-like neck to help prevent teeth from getting stained by the iron in the water.

Every day in Krynica we went on a hike in the woods for half a day. Grandma would sit on a log reading or working crossword puzzles while I played in the mountain stream catching frogs. I was crazy about frogs.

We spent afternoons in the heart of the spa drinking mineral water on the main boulevard. We would visit the bookstore and the library and buy papers from a newsstand. I was reading a lot of books about the American West. Grandma bought me a series of postcards about nature: birds of paradise from New Guinea, sea shells, African mammals, etc.

We would take a cog train to the top of Góra Parkowa (Park Mountain) and walk back down. There was a "wild" mineral spring near the top.

At night we would play cards—war, blackjack, and poker.

We would also take excursions further afield. We went to the ancient Wieliczka salt mine, a UNESCO World Heritage site. Grandma, in her mid-seventies, walked for hours in the maze of the underground tunnels and chambers full of salt sculptures. She said she did not feel at all tired.

In the evening she cracked dirty and scatological jokes with a guy from Silesia. Some of them were embarrassingly bad—like the one about two guys who shat in each other's pants.

Grandma exercised every night. Her routine included touching the ground without bending knees. She also did high kicks. Even at this age she could raise her legs above her head. Grandma exercised into her eighties. Later, the doctor asked her to abandon certain exercises. I think exercise and lots of tea kept her healthy. She also avoided sugar and cigarettes even though at that time many people, including women, smoked. Intellectual stimulation, reading, and crossword puzzles kept her mind alert.

Grandma had osteoarthritis and used a special kind of ointment with real snake venom. She also used some other natural and herbal remedies and was quite knowledgeable about them.

One day Grandma bought some mortadella (bologna sausage). I smelled it and did not like it. Grandma gave me a hard time for scorning the food.

She set an example and ate some bologna herself. Later, as usual, we went to the forest where Grandma sat down on a log to read. Then she suddenly passed out. I brought some water from the stream to revive her. When she came to, she went behind a bush and, in her own words, "did it on both ends." She threw up and had diarrhea. After that she felt better. Later she would tell the story about how I "saved her."

Grandma always got mad about people wasting food. She remembered the hunger during WWII and she hated wastefulness.

She said one should never throw away stale bread. One should feed it to the birds or grind it and use it for meatballs.

Grandma's Anecdote: St. Anthony

Grandma told me a story about a woman who was looking for a husband. She looked in vain for years. She would pray to a small statue of St. Anthony, patron saint of lost things. One day she got angry and said: "St. Anthony, you're useless!" and threw the statue through the window.

A man was passing by and was hit in the head. He ran upstairs to return the statue. That's how they met. They lived happily ever after.

Wild Piglets
Poland, 1970s

Grandma and I spent one summer vacation at a small house in the village of Halin. I was maybe eight. The house stood near a pond surrounded by weeping willows. In the evening, the frogs sang in a chorus. The water came from a deep well. One day I threw a live frog into the well, and our hosts spent several hours fishing it out. Grandma was quite permissive.

While we were there they had a wild boar hunt. They killed a sow that had two little piglets. The piglets were taken to the farm and kept in a small fenced courtyard. Unlike domestic piglets, they were hairy and striped, and they were very playful. They were also voracious eaters. When I stuck my toes through the fence, they would nibble on them and make grunting noses. "Wait till they grow up," Grandma said. This was when she told me the previously recounted story about the boar hunt.

Sex Education
Poland, 1970s

I must have been eleven or twelve when Grandma told me the story of an army officer, his wife, and their dog. It was quite a story to tell to a twelve-year-old kid.

There was this officer who had a beautiful wife and a big dog. One evening he was coming back home from the barracks. When he reached his house, he saw a couple of kids standing on tiptoe looking through the window into his bedroom. When they saw him, they ran away. He took their place by the windowsill and looked inside. His wife was naked in the bedroom having sex with their dog.

He stormed into the house, pulled out his service revolver, shot the dog, shot his wife, and blew his brains out.

This was one of many such stories Grandma recounted. She also told another one about how her male friend got raped under a shower. At first he struggled. Then he realized he enjoyed it. This is how he found out he was gay. She told me some people are that way. She told me such women are called lesbians.

I promptly shared my knowledge in school. I told my friend Paul that a woman who loves other women is a "lisbian." The teacher heard me, and she blushed.

Grandma told me another story about a masochist who had an orgasm after he was hanged. They found semen in his pants when they lowered his body from the gallows.

She told me she had a girlfriend whose nipples were so big she was ashamed to go to the beach in a swimming costume.

She told me about sensuous drawings of women by Maja Berezowska. This is the kind of art she liked most.

When I was seven or eight, we were waiting in line at a drugstore. There was a note on the wall: "We sell contraceptives."

"What are contraceptives?" I asked Grandma.

Before she had a chance to answer a middle-aged woman said: "That's heart medicine." Grandma said nothing.

When we left the drugstore Grandma said: "This woman is silly. Contraceptives, for example condoms, prevent pregnancy." Thus I learned at an early age that sex and sexuality are normal, casual conversation topics.

It got me in trouble in Poland and even more so in America, where Victorian and puritan attitudes towards sex still persist.

Grandma's Recipes: Bird in Clay

Here is a recipe for roasting a bird without plucking the feathers, which Grandma claimed she had learned from some village boys. You kill a bird, say, a partridge, with a sling. You wrap the bird in clay. You put it in a bonfire and leave it for a while between hot embers. Then you take it out and break the crust. The feathers, embedded in dry clay, easily peel from the skin while the inside is already thoroughly cooked. The bird goes well with potatoes, also baked in the bonfire.

Grandma's Joke: A Story with a Moral

The teacher asked the pupils: "Could you tell me a story with a moral?"

Little Itzak, a Jewish kid, said: "I have one. It was cold and snowing. A little sparrow was freezing. Then a horse came by and accidentally covered him with his manure. The hot horse manure kept the sparrow warm while the indigested oats provided him with food. He became very happy and started chirping. A cat heard the chirping and ate the sparrow."

"What a silly story," the teacher said. "Where is the moral?"

"There are three morals to this story," Itzak said. "Not everybody who shits on you is your enemy. Not everybody who pulls you out of the shit is your friend. When you are happy and comfortable be quiet and don't advertise it."

Grandma learned a lot of those jokes from a Jewish friend who survived the Holocaust.

Grandma's Metaphors

I was in the bathroom reading a book. I was there for a while. Grandma hollered from the anteroom: "What are you doing in there? Did you swallow a rope or something?"

When something was slow and painful, she would say, "It comes out like blood from a broken nose."

One of the colors of her palette was "diarrhea yellow." For example she would say: "Your shirt is diarrhea yellow."

When I did not feel well, she would say, "You look like shit in the grass" or "like a buttock from behind a bush."

One of her conversational gems was "You have the look of a cat shitting in the woods during a hailstorm."

Defiance
Warsaw, 1984

Granma's stories had a huge influence on how I viewed the world as a child and as a teenager.

When I was in elementary school, the teacher asked us if we wanted to join the Polish–Soviet Friendship Society. All kids signed up, not quite knowing what to expect. Remembering Grandma's stories about the Soviet invasion of 1939, about Katyń, I emphatically said "No." The teacher paid my fee out of her own pocket. This is how all children became members.

Here is my other story. The third of May, 1984, was a beautiful, sunny day. I was in high school. I was coming back from my other Grandma's house. The third of May used to be a national holiday celebrating the Polish constitution, as I said before, the world's second or third oldest codified democratic constitution (following the U.S. and perhaps Iceland). The Communists did not celebrate it—they preferred May first, the International Workers' Day. But the streets of Warsaw were full of Solidarity union members and young people, demanding freedom of speech, religion, and expression, and the freedom to organize.

I decided not to take a bus but to walk across the city to see what was going on. Even at the outskirts where my paternal grandmother lived, I could smell the tear gas. The smell of phenacyl chloride is not altogether unpleasant at low concentrations. At high concentrations it "creates an environment unbearable to humans." This is what I learned from a label on a cartridge I once stole from the police testing range.

As I approached the center of the city, the battle was in full swing. There were riot police with helmets, shields, submachine guns, armored cars, and water cannons; people were throwing stones and bottles. I decided to go down the escarpment and toward the river. As I passed a gas station, the police launched a tear gas grenade toward the group of people I was in. I kicked it back to where it came from and ran.

Soon I came across a young kid walking in the opposite direction with a heavy wooden stick. "Did you see any Communists up there?" he demanded.

"Sure," I said, "with machine guns! What do you want to accomplish with this stick?" He did not answer but continued on his way.

I reached the river's bank and mixed with another crowd of demonstrators. Now all I had to do to get home was cross the lawn under the escarpment. I was surprised not to see any people there, either police or demonstrators. Halfway across the lawn I realized what had happened. The police were on top of the escarpment with machine guns ready. I did not know they had just shot a guy in the thigh. Nobody dared approach them.

I failed to notice the blood that was still on the grass. I only saw the yellow dandelions.

I was thinking of turning back but then I thought, "Screw it! I am not going to run anymore!" I kept on walking. I was trying not to look up, but my eyes were fixed on one cop who leveled his AK-47 at my head. I could see the black muzzle of the submachine gun. I knew it carried seventy-five rounds of 7.62-mm ammo in a boatlike clip. If it was in the automatic mode, it could blow my head off. "This is it!" I thought, "I am going to die!"

I knew that some of those guys would not hesitate to kill me. Only a year earlier, also in May, Grzegorz Przemyk, a student from my high school, was beaten to death at the police station only a five minute walk from where I was at the moment. He was two days short of his nineteenth birthday. The police would direct their blows to the stomach. The idea was to destroy internal organs without leaving bruises. I went to his funeral. I wore a black ribbon in my lapel all the way back home from the funeral, even though the police were everywhere, and such a display might end up in another vicious beating.

Going back to my story, this time I did not feel normal fear, fear of the unknown. I felt anger, helplessness, and defiance. I could feel the hair on the back of my head and neck stand up on end. I kept walking. The whole moment must have lasted only seconds, but to me it was like eternity.

Then I saw one of the other cops, perhaps an officer, grab the barrel of the other cop's AK-47 and point it to the ground. I heard him say, "What are you doing, you idiot?" Five minutes later I was home.

Food Stories
Poland, 1980s

In the early 1980s, during and after the time of martial law, the food was rationed in Poland again, as it had been during WWII.

We saw exotic food such as oranges and bananas and famous Polish cold cuts, smoked ham and smoked sirloin (similar to Canadian bacon), only about twice a year on Christmas and Easter.

At that time retired Polish grandmothers became national heroes patiently waiting in lines to buy bread, potatoes, or meat. Grandma Maria, now almost eighty, was one of them. She would bring home a bag full of basic products as well as something fancy for me or my sister, for example a chocolate-like confection that contained no real chocolate.

Sometimes she bought us some horse meat, which wasn't rationed. When I first came to America and mentioned I had eaten horse meat, somebody said to me, "In this country we don't eat horses!"

Poland has a long tradition of horsemanship, and Grandma was a horse lover herself. But when it came to feeding a hungry family, those purely cultural and personal preferences became unimportant.

Before WWII Poland had a booming free-market economy with a brand-new seaport in Gdynia, good universities, and a strong currency. Grandma Maria told us that, back then, one could have a dinner at a restaurant for one Polish *złoty*. Now similar things cost hundreds of *złotys*, then thousands, and soon millions. Most people could not afford dining out at all.

She told us about food like shrimp, lobster, caviar, oysters, things I had never seen in my life. She said Grandpa Johnny liked to suck oysters after putting some lemon juice on them. She told us the best part of the lobster is the tail. I first saw the foods Grandma had talked about in America in 1984. I recognized them from her stories.

Grandma lived long enough to see the fall of Communism, to see the stores full once again, and to enjoy some of the food she remembered from her youth.

Grandma's Legacy

Grandma Maria had a great influence on my upbringing. As I said before, we spent several vacations together, just the two of us. While other kids went to summer camps I was the grandma's boy. She was an important role model.

She incited my curiosity about the world by talking about faraway places like China. Eventually, I would visit almost fifty countries on five continents and see with my own eyes things Grandma told me about.

Speaking to me in four or five languages, she encouraged me to learn several on my own. She made the use of multiple languages normal and acceptable. Some things were simply easier to phrase in this language or that.

Curious about everything, she often talked about science and technology. For example, she told me about early radios that came with headsets; they had no loudspeakers. She also told me about the prewar super-train called *Lukstorpeda*. It was so fast one could get dizzy looking through the window when the train was in motion.

She talked about cameras so small they could be hidden in a ring. She was sometimes exaggerating, but some of her exaggerations later became reality. She demonstrated how to tell real amber from fake. She would rub a piece of amber to produce a static electric charge and pick up pieces of paper clinging to it. Or she would heat it up and let me "smell the pine forest." Those stories and demonstrations may have encouraged me to become an engineer and an inventor.

I learned from Grandma a kind of scatological humor that often got me into trouble.

Most of all, I learned persistence in the face of adversity that helped me a lot as an immigrant in America. Like Grandma in Germany, I found myself surrounded by a different culture. Like

Grandma, despite my education, I had to do physical labor to survive.

I also learned from Grandma a certain degree of defiance that got me into more trouble, first with the Communist authorities in Poland, then in America. She taught me that if the rules are unreasonable they should be broken.

Grandma provided me with a moral backbone. She taught me not to lie except in very unusual circumstances. She taught me to help others without expecting anything in return and to tolerate and try to understand people who were different from me. She instilled in me the contempt for material possessions and status symbols.

Grandma was the first to read books to me, and she set me on a lifelong path of reading. As I said before, she also bought me my first camera. Photography became another passion of mine.

Grandma encouraged my life habits: exercising, drinking black tea and coffee, never wasting food, occasionally indulging in life's little pleasures, but almost always in moderation.

Bottle of Wine
Warsaw, 1992

**Grandma with her vodka and pink carnations,
Christmas 1991**

The last time I saw Grandma Maria was on Christmas of 1991. I had come over from the U.S. As always, she went to the hair stylist to, in her own words, "turn myself into a goddess." As always, she drank her vodka during the traditional Christmas Eve supper.

I was to come back in the summer of 1992. I announced it to my mom in winter. Grandma Maria, however, said she was not going to live until the summer. She told my mom where she kept my favorite wine so that, when I came to visit, I could have it. She also gave instructions about her finances and everything else. She was completely lucid and composed. She told my sister Eva she was going to look after her from heaven.

She died in the spring of 1992, few months short of her ninetieth birthday. She died quietly in her bed holding a picture of Father Pio, her favorite religious figure. My mom was at her side almost to the end.

At one point Grandma, weak and exhausted, suddenly became her old, energetic self. She said in a strong voice, "I want you to leave now. I don't want you to see this." This was the last time my mother saw her alive.

Suggested Reading

Norman Davies, *God's Playground: A History of Poland*, Columbia University Press, New York, 1982

Adam Zamoyski, *The Polish Way, A Thousand-year history of the Poles and their Culture*, Franklin Watts, New York – Toronto, 1988

B. M. Szonert, *World War II Through Polish Eyes*, East European Monographs, Boulder (distributed by Columbia University Press), 2002

Witold Rybczynski, *My Two Polish Grandfathers*, Scribner, New York, 2009

Bohdan Arct, *Prisoner of War, My secret journal*, Polwen, Radom, 2002

Wladyslaw Szpilman, *The Pianist*, Picador, New York, 2003

Gerda Weissmann Klein, *All But My Life*, Hill and Wang, New York, 1995

Rutka Laskier, *Rutka's Notebook: A voice from the Holocaust*, Yad Vashem, 2008

The Permanent Book of The 20th Century, Carroll & Graf Publishers, Inc., New York, 1994

Eyewitness to History, Avon Books, New York, 1990